Christmas at Downtown

Holiday Foods and Tradition from the Unofficial Guide to Downtown Abbey

Elizabeth Fellow

Elizabeth Fellow

Table of Contents

Welcome to Christmas at Downton Abbey

Look across the Yorkshire Moors to the Abbey on Christmas day. Surrounded by trees, the branches glisten in the crisp, freezing frost. From the windows, the golden glow of warmth dances across the snow. Inside, the Crawleys and their household prepare to unveil their most spectacular Christmas yet.

For the first time this year, you are invited to join the feast. Enjoy a privileged insight into the Downton Abbey Christmas and the preparations that made it so fine.

Experiment with some of their glorious food of the period, from the glamorous Charlotte Russe and Consommé with quails eggs to the ancient traditional mince pie containing real chunks of beef.

Hold the perfect Christmas party, with instructions from how the table should be laid right through to which drinks should be served.

So without further ado, don your most beautiful frock and pearls, style your hair, and put on your gloves. Because, we ladies.... are off to Downton Abbey to enjoy Christmas in quite the most elegant style.

Elizabeth Fellow

What Yorkshire was REALLY like in 1920s

The Downton Abbey Christmas Special always marks the pinnacle of the festive season's TV. Larger than life, the Specials always sparkle with brilliant story lines and elegant visual delights. The 2012 episode was reputed to have cost a mouth-watering £12 million to create. While that seems to be an inordinate production bill, it is in line with the mountainous cost of a Christmas celebration in English stately home in the 1920s.

The Christmas meal was the very largest of all statements of wealth. It was an opportunity for the Lord and Lady to showcase their achievements not only in financial terms of the harvest of their lands, but in their personal success as a marriage and family unit too.

As the 2014 season opens, we see the attitudes of the British towards their beloved aristocracy beginning to falter. The clever introduction of Tom Branson, the emergent ambassador for the proletariat just as a labour government comes into power, means we shall likely see changes in the dynamic of the household over the coming seasons. Already we can feel Carson's discomfort of the class divide starting to dissolve.

Downton is set in the breath taking scenery of Yorkshire, one of the most northerly counties of England. Summers are clement, bright, and airy. Winters are bitterly cold and extremely harsh. Christmas days glisten with biting frosts.

A hundred years prior, Emily Bronte had described Yorkshire's stark landscape far better than I ever could in her immortal book *Wuthering Heights*. Having witnessed Yorkshire's changing seasons every day of her life, she is magically able to transport us there with her words.

7

She vividly paints pictures of the "golden rocks" of
Penistone Crags, black hollows, bleak hilltops, bilberry
bushes, moonlit scenery, miles of heath, and winding roads.
The Yorkshire moors are a stark and frankly, unnerving place.
It is cold, blustery, and wet. In the dark days of winter, it is
easy to get lost, especially when the snow does come down.

On this dark landscape stood the strong fortress of
Downton Abbey. Inside, fires crackled, candles burned,
chandeliers glinted. The soft devoré fabrics of Lady
Grantham's dresses shimmered in the softened light. Her
sequinned evening wear, beaded to within an inch of its life,
sparkled and glistened in its warmth. Beds were warmed with
copper bedpans fuelled by burning embers. As dusk stole the
last moments of light, a golden glow of wealth radiates into
the gloom, extinguished only by heavy curtains drawn to keep
out the cold. These great draughty houses were massive
sources of employment. Of course, like any business, as the
house flourished, it grew, and so (very slightly) did the
fortunes of those living on the estates. When we look at
records contemporaneous to the period, we can see just how
much commerce passed through their doors.

At Welbeck Abbey, in Nottinghamshire, the Duke of
Portland employed more than 60 staff inside of his house. A
further 200 were employed in the stables, gardens, and home
farm. In fact, records show that the Welbeck Abbey Annual
Servants Ball was so grand an affair that a massive 50 waiters
had to be seconded in from London to serve the crowd of
workers.

A wonderful old record from Longleat (now the
home of a Safari Park) gives us some insights into some of
the jobs our modern day minds might struggle to imagine.
The Marquis of Bath of the day, similar in spirit to our own
Dowager Duchess, refused to install electricity purely on
grounds of taste. Therefore, her household employed a young

man whose job title was that of "lamp boy." His endless task was to clean, trim, and refill Longleat's 400 oil lamps (plus the 140 candles in the private chapel). Because this role seemed not to entirely fill his day, each evening, 60 pairs of shoes were also laid out for him to polish.

Today, a workforce of more than 250 staff would be considered an impressively large business. Yet this was simply the workings of one stately home. Employment in the great houses was deemed to be an honour and a very good job. A regular wage coming in to a servant's home was very welcome. Also, servants ate pretty well.

Later we will explore some of the dishes which would have been served on Christmas day. The "upstairs" menu was lavish and indulgent, starting with a breakfast of kedgeree or perhaps of brawn, a light lunch of Game Pie, and then afternoon tea. Christmas dinner would be a belt-busting six courses, which included a starter, a fish dish, the turkey dinner (because turkeys were the most expensive birds you could buy), and dessert, cheese, and fruit courses.

When you consider the price of the food, that bill is expensive. Then you can factor in the wages of the staff. There would likely be more seconded in to manage the needs of visitors, and of course, simple tasks like lighting and tending fires. Those tending the fires had to then clean out the grates, so that they would be ready for the next fire, an inordinate amount of labour. Not to mention of course…the washing up?

So the question is, where on earth did the money come from?

There was a strange symbiosis between England's great houses and their tenants. The bills of the house were met by the rent paid by the tenants of the estate, most of whom worked for the great house anyway. So there was this circle of money going in and out in an endless spiral. By the 1870s though, a depression in agricultural prices meant that houses like Downton Abbey were beginning to struggle. The bills to run the houses, let alone heat them, were vast, and most houses had a shortfall in their coffers.

To many houses, women like our beautiful Cora held the secret to survival.

Late in the 19th Century, the fast ocean liners began to bring the lifeline from America. The so called "Dollar Princesses" were beautiful, articulate, bright, but most of all…loaded. Turning their backs on American society, they headed across the Atlantic to bag themselves a prince. When struggling English landowners met up with these glamorous, rich beauties, wedding bells usually began to chime. In all, between 1870 and the breakout of the Great War, 350 Dollar Princesses took up English titles.

On the surface, their steely determination to marry into a castle seems crass and unpleasant, but the matches made perfect commercial sense. Americans had money, and then some! The Wall Street Crash was still half a decade away, and in typically English style, envy was smothered by a stiff upper lip. The British watched agog as the Manhattan skyscrapers grew taller, and the geometric art deco façade got ever shinier. How could skint landowners in the draughty English countryside fail to be impressed? Of course, they wanted a piece of it. Who on earth wouldn't?!

The injection of cash these marriages brought into the British economy is believed to have amounted to over a billion dollars. That's one hell of a Christmas lunch. With their dowries and huge travelling coffers, they brought with them some of the most "unsavoury characteristics." Just imagine Yorkshire girls' faces when the foreigners followed the men into the drawing room for a game of cards, and giggled out loud instead of stifling their laughter behind their hands.

These tomboy, ladette traits were not their only gifts to today's society. Just twenty years later, in 1940, England was extremely grateful for one of these marriages, when the son of a Dollar Princess became Prime Minister. Winston Churchill of course, went on to lead England and her allies to win the Second World War. Princess Diana too, descended from one of these unions. Her Great-Grandmother, Frances Ellen Work, had been a wealthy New York socialite who married James Roche, 3rd Baron Femoy.

So while the heyday of the Anglo-American marriage alliance was over by 1923, we can imagine the party to be bustling with transatlantic energy. There would be some Yorkshire drawl in the drawing room, but more likely London chatter spiced with some American charm too. What's for sure is that no party was just a party. This is where associations and lobbying commenced.

At parties, these beautiful women were strategically invited, by the likes of the Dowager Duchess, to create a buzz. They were an irresistible societal draw, almost like speed dating for the upper classes. Every Lord wanted to get close to these glamorous and savvy women, and I feel sure the English ladies were loath to miss an opportunity to check out the competition. Instinct tells me too, that the steely females had to have pretty thick skins not to get pricked by the thorny English Roses.

While family and friends would just have likely held their allure as they do today, the promise of a Christmas celebration of Downton scale would have to be strong to tempt people from their London homes to the bitter North.

The menu had to be extraordinary, and the "show" without compare.

Today we follow the trends of magazines for Christmas themes to set our own stages, but in England in 1924, there would have been one resounding theme. In February of the previous year, Howard Carter had opened the tomb of Tutankhamen, on a trip financed by the Earl of Caernarvon, the owner of Highclere Castle, Downton Abbey's true-life form. England was in love with anything golden and sparkly, beguiled by the charm of Ancient Egyptian tales.

The previous year the Prince of Wales had also married his lifelong love Elizabeth Bowes-Lyon in Westminster Abbey. At this point, of course, no one could even have dreamed that there might be the abdication of Edward VII (in 1936 because of his association with an American divorcée!), and that Prince would eventually become King. The change in fortunes for George VI and Queen Elizabeth meant they became parents to one of England's greatest monarchs.

Everything was understatedly extravagant as the country celebrated their royalty and that of the Pharaohs. The British Empire had never been stronger. Records from '22 showed the Empire ruled over 458 million people. That was one fifth of the planet's population. The gunfire of the Great War was long behind them, and England celebrated.

So, what would Christmas spectacle of this magnitude have looked and tasted like?

Christmas in a Stately Home

The splendour of the occasion would have been incredible. Central to the décor was, of course, the Christmas tree. Filling the hall with the scent of pine counterpointed with cinnamon, oranges, and nutmegs of the garlands, it was a festive welcome to guests. Great balustrades and fireplaces of the period were swathed with fresh branches and fruits brought in from the garden. Candlelight glints in glass baubles hung all around. Pomegranates, orange pomanders stuck with cloves, and garlands were all beautiful and welcome reminders of British Christmases right back to the Romans. This invisible thread to generations past filled the house with nostalgia and hope.

In our Downton Abbey, Carson and his footmen work industriously throughout the day, laying the festive table. Constructed with geometric precision, the men create a vision of crystal and porcelain splendour. Gracing the centre of the table are carefully thought-out decorations. Getting this part correct is central to the success of the host. Table settings are elegantly streamlined. Huge candelabras, spread along the length of the table, bathe the room in golden light. Mirrored plateaus (very like the stands we place the bottom tier of a wedding cake on today) are vital to establishing the rhythm of the decoration. Tall candlesticks alternate with lower floral decorations, making it far easier for the guests to talk. In each candlestick is a white taper candle, carefully chosen to be just taller than its housing stick.

Amidst cut glass and gleaming silver lay walnuts wrapped in red ribbons. These traditional Christmas favourites had been already cracked and then had the nut replaced, the ribbons securing them fast. It simply wouldn't do to mess the table with shards of shell.

Crisp, perfectly pressed, white linen covers the table. Subtly delineating each place setting, or correctly termed "cover" is a strand of ivy, or a line of delicate flowers. Each place is laid carefully, ensuring the traditional cutlery etiquette is observed.

To create the splendid luxury of the Christmas table was a feat of expert calculation and precision in these stately homes. It was necessary to place each setting equidistant apart. Each cover was correctly placed between 24-30 inches away from the last. A last-minute, unexpected guest could create a huge amount of extra work and movement behind the scenes, to maintain this necessary standard.

At each place was laid a service plate, exactly one inch from the edge of the table. It would remain there until replaced by a hot plate. Stacked on top was each of the plates in the order in which they would be required. To the left of the plate were placed the forks required for the meal, tines up. The guests would work through the courses from outside to in. To avoid clumsiness, the central fork (that of the entrée), was laid slightly higher than the other two, so it nestled neatly between them both. The order then was entrée, fish, meat course. Salad or dessert forks were not laid in the setting, but rather brought to the table with the course. Above these was placed the bread plate, with the butter knife laid across and to the side of the plate. To the right were the knives for the meat (inside), fish (middle), and any h'ors d'euvres or fruit spoons (outermost). Again, the handle of each item of cutlery was placed exactly one inch from the edge of the table.

It had recently become *de rigeur* to serve a different beverage with each course. Any oyster course was to be accompanied by Chablis, soups and hot hors d'œuvres would be partnered with sherry, and fish with hock. Champagne was enjoyed with entrées (the starter course) and removes (the main course), meat with burgundy, game with claret, and dessert with port and other fine wines. Consequently, glass placement had become quite complex too. The water glass was placed just above the meat knife, champagne and sherry in line with the hors d'oeuvres spoon.

Starched white napkins were laid to the left, with the hem and selvedge parallel to the edge of the table and the forks. At each place was a menu (written in French) with the intended diner's name, indicating the seating of the guests her Ladyship felt most suitable.

Her planning of the event would have held great importance because dinner parties were key to one's acceptance and rise through society. Whilst Downton is already a well-respected and thriving business concern, networking held the key to its future existence.

And yet, business is such a bore, don't you think? One simply doesn't speak politics or religion at the table. Conversation should be twinkling and light. So how would the Countess have known who to invite? The perfect dinner party guest list had a well-respected formula. An equal number of guests, ideally with two more gentlemen than ladies, made entrance to the dining room as graceful an execution as it could be.

So, as the bell chimes the signal of the first guests, Carson readies himself to meet them at the door. Dinner is served between eight and nine, and etiquette dictates arriving between 15 and 30 minutes before dining.

In the States, since around 1910, cocktails had become fashionable before dining, and had become very much the way in the fashionable houses. However in an early episode of Season 5, a guest mischievously asks Mary, "Shouldn't we be having cocktails?" To this, Mary quips, "I

think it will be a long time before we see those at Downton!"
You may also notice the slight deviation of the "rule" that
men stand and women sit in the drawing room before dinner.
Not less than 15 years before, that would have categorically
been set in stone. Yet, one can see that these are the
beginning of the emancipation years, and already the beautiful
frocks can be seen circulating the room.

The guests mingle until the last invitee has arrived,
and the procession to the dining room commences. Since the
reign of William IV, it has been traditional that the guests
enter the room in pairs. The highest ranking women were
partnered by gentlemen, whilst the lower ranked entered
alone, should there not be enough men to go round! The
extra gentlemen chosen by the Countess were to alleviate the
embarrassment of the senior ladies all having to go into the
room with each other's husbands....

At Downton, as the guests enter the room, not only is
it beautiful, twinkling in the candlelight, it is immaculately set.
Each chair is pulled out exactly a foot and a half away from
the table, in readiness for the butler and footmen to help the
ladies in. The fragrance of the melting wax, the vision of the
candied Satsumas on the table, and the warming decanters of
red wine fill the room, undoubtedly making the guests'
mouths water in anticipation of what is to come.

His Lordship and his escorted lady sit at the bottom
of the table, with the second ranking woman to his left. Men
and ladies alternate the circumference of the table.

Over the next few hours, the table will groan under
the lavish feast of so many dishes. In total, the revellers will
eat their way through a massive six courses, each more
intricately prepared than the last. Every course requires
attention to detail, colourful presentation, and has to be a

feast for the eyes. It should be every bit as sensory as the taste.

The entrée, or as we would now less glamorously call it, the starter, was potentially the most fulfilling for the kitchen to make. It would predominately be made from what we would now dismiss as offal, the cheaper off cuts and innards of the beast. In English society of the period, this was considered to be the very height of luxury. The challenge for the kitchen, then, would be to make a delicacy of very raw ingredients. Liver, kidney, and brains of the beast were prepared in a hundred different ways to excite the taste buds of the guests. These ingredients had to compare on an even footing to the luxury of the expensive great bird.

This dish would be a riot of colour, usually created by greens of herbs, reds of tomatoes perhaps, and usually served with potatoes.

As a child growing up in England in the seventies, I was fascinated by copper moulds that one would see in thrift shops. I found it extremely odd that someone might want to make a jelly in the form of a fish! (In actual fact, I suspect I also thought the jelly might taste of fish too, and I really didn't fancy that at all!) In fact, these beautifully ornate coppers were part of the cook's arsenal for creating fish mousses for the table. (I am more comfortable now I know that, but am kicking myself for not having collected the cookware when it was so cheap!!!)

The fish dish would have been caught on the estate of the house. Thus, in Yorkshire it would be rainbow trout, brown trout, salmon, or greyling. Freshly brought from the river to the kitchen, it would be poached, flaked, and creamed into a concoction by Mrs. Patmore, and then moulded into glorious and impressive shapes. The largest salmon though, were poached and served whole at the table, head and tails intact and were decorated with the most slender slices of cucumber arranged to look like scales. The glaze of the aspic gave the beautiful creature the sheen of its life in the water.

The main course, or remove, on Christmas day was always Turkey, upstairs, at Downton Abbey. It was a costly specimen and the ultimate status symbol to be able to afford such extravagance. Most usually grown on the estate, and fattened through the year, the bird was a great showpiece of farming.

Whilst you and I might imagine this enormous bird as the centrepiece of the table, because of the restrictions of the oven size, there may have been several smaller birds lining the table. Whilst upstairs would enjoy a turkey, downstairs would be looking forward to a goose. The bird, just as it is today, would be surrounded by an array of vegetables. Some of the vegetables we recognise as "ordinary" ingredients, like duchess potatoes, glazed carrots, and sprouts and chestnuts, were dressed up in their Christmas best. Other vegetables that have gone out of fashion now, like endives and cardoons, would also have completed the spread.

In exactly the same way as the entrées were made from entrails, any leftovers from the vegetables would be collected up for Boxing Day soup. Cabbage and sprouts would be made up into "bubble and squeak," a traditional English dish made with the leftover vegetables. Whilst the meal was in every way lavish, it was by no means wasteful.

Dessert was the climax of the Christmas meal, with a wide range of options available. I'm sure opinion was split, as it is today, with some loving the Christmas Pudding and others preferring a lighter choice. As the pudding entered the room alight, blue flames danced magically over the surface of its dome.

The meal would end with cheese and biscuits. Everyone would then retire for coffee and truffles.

In Victorian times, it would have been customary for the hostess to incline her head to the lady of next rank as a signal that they should retire. By '24, such formalities had been dispensed with, but on such an occasion as Christmas, it seems likely the men would enjoy a game of cards whilst the ladies withdrew for a game of charades.

As the evening drew on, after crackers had been pulled and everyone was becoming more than a little tipsy, a tune would be struck on the piano. All gathered round the great Christmas tree to sing carols and Christmas songs.

A long night, I would suggest, because by the twenties, there were no rules about what time guests should leave. Warm by the fire, conversation drifted on to early morn.

Downstairs, can you imagine how tired they would have been?

Each part of the meal had been placed in a porcelain or earthenware dish. These heavy servers had been carried, one by one, travelling up a flight of stairs and along a long corridor. Even the slightest tip of the sauces could spoil the servants' immaculately clean gloves, throwing the conveyor belt of service into complete disarray. The valets had carefully circulated the table in a clockwise direction, serving each guest in turn. They had been careful not to make eye contact with the diners and to speak only when spoken to. Their humble service was like a well-oiled machine.

The air downstairs would have felt entirely different to the dining room, still warm, but damp and steamy. All would have been relieved that the dinner has been so well received. Where upstairs the scents are pine-ey, melting candle wax-y, and wine-y, downstairs the air, a far more delicious aroma, filled with cinnamon, nutmeg, brown sugar, and treacle would have pervaded.

After the diners left, and the servants had cleared the table away, the butler would attend to the guests upstairs. At that point, a start is made for the servants' festivities to begin. Most years the servants would not eat until gone 11 o'clock. They must, of course, rise again the next morning at five. The refectory, bedecked in paper chains and baubles, would be a gloriously bright and colourful occasion.

The servants table was by no means meagre. On top of their goose masterpiece would be titbits from the table upstairs, extras having been made to ensure enough to go round. Drinks too could not be wasted. A different wine served with every course meant a fairly sloshed servants quarter too.

When they finally retire, Carson, Mrs. Hughes, Mrs. Patmore, and the staff are warm, contented, and more than just a little bit tired. They can be very proud of their work, for they have done the house proud. It was a masterpiece of culinary showmanship. Please allow me introduce you now to the dishes of the day.

Christmas Breakfast

Upstairs the family would eat a large breakfast, very different in nature to what we would expect now. A traditional Christmas day favourite was Brawn.

Brawn

This is an impressive and tasty dish, made by very frugal ingenuity on Mrs. Patmore's part. Any good English housekeeper had a good Brawn recipe hidden inside of her apron. This rich dish uses all the parts of the pig left over from a roast pork dinner, and so, in effect, is free food. The butcher is happy to sell this "offal" very cheaply indeed. If you are a little squeamish, speak to your butcher about preparing the joints as follows below.

The 1920's was the decade of Aspic, everything was suspended in glistening, translucent jelly. This recipe, however, utilises the natural gelatine hiding inside of the pig's trotters.

Ingredients:

- 1 Pig's head (remove the cheeks and ears and quarter them)
- 4 pig's trotters (pig's feet)
- 1 pig's tail
- 1 bulb chopped fennel
- 3 finely sliced carrots
- 3 finely sliced shallots
- 1 sprig chopped sage

- 1 sprig lemon thyme
- Celery salt, to taste
- 1 lemon, juice only
- 6 bay leaves, for garnishing

Directions:

1. Take a blowtorch to the pig's head to ensure all of the hairs are removed.

2. Place everything, all meat and vegetables, into a large saucepan of boiling water. Simmer for 24 hours, then leave it to cool in the cooking juices.

3. Drain off (retain the juices in a jug), and then remove all the meat. Chop it finely, and transfer it to a bowl.

4. Add the fennel, carrot, and shallots back in with the meat.

5. Stir in the herbs, season with celery salt, and mix everything together.

6. Use the bay leaves to decorate the bottom of a serving bowl, and then spoon the meat onto the leaves.

7. Drizzle the lemon juice evenly over the meat, and then ladle the cooking liquid over the mix.

8. To get the very best brawn, the meat needs to be packed very tightly. Mrs. Patmore would have placed

a plate on top and used a 1lb (454g) weight from her scales. A tin of beans works just as well!!

9. Refrigerate for 12 hours until set, and serve with new potatoes or crusty bread

Kedgeree

Another frugal masterpiece, this time using leftover fish. Ay fish works well, but smoked haddock has a particularly lovely tang.

Ingredients:

- 1 lb (454g) (roughly) any cooked fish
- ¼ lb (125g) rice
- 1 hardboiled egg
- 3 oz (75g) butter
- 1 tsp parsley
- Cayenne pepper and salt

Directions:

1. Boil the rice until soft.
2. Flake the fish finely.
3. Melt the butter in a skillet, and gently fry off the fish and rice over a fairly hot burner.
4. Should the mixture seem too dry, add a splash of milk.
5. Chop the egg white. Pass the yolk through a sieve to make a brightly coloured powder.
6. Add the white of the egg to the mix
7. Season to taste.
8. Serve on a hot dish, and pile your mix really high.

9. Garnish with the bright yellow yolk and oodles of chopped fresh parsley.

The Holiday Luncheon

Raised Game Pie

For luncheon, just something light! This game pie is a perfect example. It had the added benefit that Mrs. Patmore could prepare this well in advance, simply serve, and get on with the masterpiece of dinner.

Whilst it looks like a massive cook, it is extremely simple and quick to make, and always garners much admiration on the table. The depth of flavour comes from extra time taken the day before, cooking in marinade and creating a delicious stock. It is made from layering pork with game rubied with port. It is held together with a lusciously rich, jellied stock.

Ingredients:

For the filling:

- 2 1/2 lb (1.25kg) game meat (use 1 1/2 lb/ 700g venison, and then top up with small game)
- 5 fl oz (150 ml)
- 2 Tbsp brandy
- 1/2 level tsp dried thyme
- butter, for greasing,
- 1 lb (454g) hard back pork fat
- 1 lb (454g) lean pork
- 1 1/4 level tsp ground ginger

- 1 1/4 level tsp ground cinnamon

- 3/4 tsp nutmeg

- 1 clove of crushed garlic

- 2-3 level tsp fresh chopped parsley

- 8 oz (225 g) thin, unsmoked bacon rashers

- salt and pepper to season

For the jellied stock:

- 4 allspice berries

- 6 whole black peppercorns

- 1 level tsp dried thyme

- 2 bay leaves

- 1 carrot

- 1 onion stuck with 4 cloves

- lemon juice

- 1/2 oz (11g) powdered gelatine

- salt

For the hot-water crust pastry:

- 1 lb 8 oz (1.3kg) plain flour

- 3 level tsp (15 ml) salt

- 6 oz (150 g) lard

- 1/4 pt (300ml) milk or milk and water

- a beaten egg to glaze

Directions:

Day 1:

1. Marinate the meat

2. Trim all the meat away from the bones, and cut into small cubes. Retain all the bones and scraps to make a lovely rich stock. Pour the port over the meat, season with salt and pepper, and add the thyme. Leave to marinate in a cool place overnight.

3. Meanwhile, make your stock:

4. Add the bones and scraps to a deep saucepan, and cover with water.

5. Add the stock herbs and spices, together with the carrot and the onion stuck with cloves.

6. Bring your concoction to the boil, and simmer it gently for 2 hours.

7. Every now and then, take a Tbsp and skim any scum off the surface of the stock.

8. Strain off the stock into a sieve.

9. Return to the saucepan, and boil rapidly until the stock reduces to just one pint. (570 ml)

10. Taste and season with salt and lemon juice as needed

11. Remove the stock from the heat, and whisk in the packet of gelatine

12. Cover and leave to chill, ready for cooking tomorrow

Day 2:

As the stock sets, any bits settle on the top. Skim these off to leave a very clear, jellied stock.

To make the hot-water pastry:

1. Mix the flour and the salt.

2. Melt the lard in the milk/water, bring to the boil, and pour into the bowl of flour.

3. Use a wooden spoon to beat the mixture quickly to form a dough.

4. Collect the mixture together, and lightly need into shape. Knead until smooth.

5. Cover with cling film, place in the refrigerator, and leave to rest for 20-30 minutes

To make the pork filling:

1. Mince the pork fat and lean pork. Mrs. Patmore would have used an old mincer clamped to the table, but we'll excuse you for using a food processor!

2. Add the garlic, parsley, and spices, with a sprinkle of salt and pepper.

3. Mix the ingredients together well, and then divide into four equal patties, each just slightly smaller than the diameter of the cake tin.

Constructing the pie:

1. Preheat your oven to 180°C / 350°F / Gas 4.

2. Divide the pastry into 1/3 for the lid, and 2/3 for the case. Rewrap the lid pastry, and place a side for the moment.

3. Roll out your pastry to big enough to line a lightly greased 18cm / 7in spring cake tin.

4. The pastry needs to come up a good 1/4-inch higher than the sides of the tin to seal the lid. Carefully check the pastry for holes and cracks. We don't want the stock to leak out!

5. Now we are going to build the pie, alternating one pork patty, then a 1/3 of the marinated meat. Repeat so there are four layers of pork and three layers of game. You should have pork on the top and on the bottom.

6. Roll out your remaining pastry to make your lid.

7. Glaze the inside of the pastry base, and place on the lid.

8. Carefully pinch the edges of the pie crust together well to give a good join and a pretty finish.

9. Cut a hole in the centre measuring about a 1 cm square, so you can add the stock, and the steam can also escape too.

10. Decorate the crust with creations of leaves, diamonds, or roses made from your pastry trimmings. Stick these on with a little egg, then glaze the top of the pie with the rest of the egg.

To cook the pie:

1. Lay a sheet of foil over the pie to prevent the top from burning.

2. Bake at 220°C / 420°F /Gas 7 for 15-20 minutes.

3. Remove the foil, and then bake at 180°C / 350°F / Gas 4 for 1 hour or until tender.

4. Gently poke a skewer through the hole to test the meat.

5. Remove from the oven, and gently remove from the cake tin (I tend to leave mine sitting on the base and just remove the sides)

6. Brush the sides of the pie with the remaining egg to get a really golden brown glaze.

7. Return to the oven and bake for 30 minutes more.

8. Remove and cool for around 10 minutes.

9. Pour the cold stock through the steam hole, a little at a time. (A funnel makes this a good deal easier.) If the cold stock has set, warm it a little until it liquefies again.

10. Leave the pie to cool completely, and top up with stock to fill the pastry if your level falls a little short.

11. Once completely cold, wrap well, and chill in the fridge until ready to serve with salad or crusty bread.

Afternoon Tea

What Christmas Day afternoon would be complete without traditional mince pies? This is a sweet version for individual pies. I have also included a Victorian recipe containing beef, which is best served as a full pie. You can find this in the desserts section.

For more ideas of cakes and pastries, see my book *Tea at Downton* (http://www.amazon.com/dp/B00I5ASVX0).

Mince Pies

Ingredients:

- 1 lb (454g) of homemade mincemeat (see below)
- 1 lb (454g) Rich shortcrust pastry
- 1 egg beaten
-

Mince Meat

This traditional mincemeat improves with age. Why not make several pots and surprise your friends?

Ingredients:

- 1 lb (454g) apples
- 1/2 lb (225g) sultanas
- 1 lb (454g) seeded raisins
- 1 lb (454g) currants
- 1 lb (454g) beef suet
- 1 lb (454g) butter (melted)
- 1/2 lb (225g) soft brown sugar
- 6 oz (170g) peel
- 1/2 oz (11g) mixed spice
- 1 tsp ground cloves
- 1 lemon
- 1 orange
- 100 ml brandy
- Salt

Directions:

1. Chop the suet very finely, and melt the butter.
2. Peel and core the apples, and grate or mince them finely.
3. Chop the sultans, raisins, currants, and peel.
4. Use the zests of the orange and lemon, and the juice of half of each.

5. Add all the ingredients to a large bowl.

6. Pour in the melted butter and brandy, and stir together well.

7. Season with the salt to taste.

8. Cover and leave in a cool place to mature for at least a week.

9. Stir regularly.

Pastry

<u>**Ingredients:**</u>

- 1 lb (454g) plain flour

- 10 oz (285g) butter

- Cold water

- Salt

<u>**Directions:**</u>

1. Chop the butter into very small pieces, then rub into the sieved flour and salt until it resembles fine breadcrumbs.

2. Gradually add in enough chilled water to make a soft dough.

3. Chill in the refrigerator for 20 minutes before using.

To make the pies:

<u>Directions:</u>

1. Preheat oven to 220°C / 420°F /Gas 8.

2. Flour a board, and roll out 2/3 of the dough to about a 1/4-inch thickness.

3. Cut out the bases to the pies. Place each one into the patty tin.

4. Fill with a Tbsp of mincemeat in each.

5. Using the beaten egg, glaze the top insides of each pie to make a glue for the lid.

6. Cut out the lids, and crimp them closed.

7. Brush over with the remaining egg.

8. Using a fork, gently skewer a hole in the middle for the steam to escape.

9. Cook in a preheated oven of 220°C / 420°F /Gas 8 for 25-30 minutes or until golden brown.

Christmas Cake

Ingredients:

- 1 lb (454g) flour
- 3/4 lb (340g) butter
- 1/2 lb (225g) sugar (castor or brown)
- 1 lb (454g) sultanas
- 1 lb (454g) currants
- 6 oz (170g) mixed peel (chopped)
- 1/4 lb (115g) glace cherries (chopped)
- 6 large eggs
- 1/4 lb (115g) blanched almonds
- 1 tsp of grated orange rind
- 1 Tbsp of black treacle
- 1 level Tbsp baking powder
- 1/2 tsp mixed spice
- 1 wineglass of brandy

Directions:

1. Preheat the oven to 180°C / 350°F / Gas 6.
2. Sieve the flour, baking powder, spices, and a pinch of salt.
3. Chop the almonds and cherries.

4. Cream together the butter and sugar until light and fluffy.

5. Add the eggs, one at a time, beating each one into the mixture well before adding the next, and add one tsp of the spiced flour mix between each.

6. Stir in the treacle.

7. Now add in the rest of the ingredients, the flour, fruit, nuts, brandy, and zest.

8. Use a metal spoon to mix, so as to avoid knocking out all of the air. Fold the ingredients together well.

9. Test the thickness of the mixture. If it feels a little heavy, add a little milk.

10. Preparing the cake tin is an intricate process, but is well worth taking the time. The cake has a long cooking time, and this will avoid any burning or dryness.

11. Use a 10-in tin.

12. Grease the inside of the tin.

13. Now take greaseproof paper and line the OUTSIDE of the tin, double thickness, so it stands about 2 inches higher than the top of the tin.

14. Secure the paper into place using string.

15. Carefully spoon your mixture into the tin.

16. If you intend to ice the cake, you may want to smooth the mixture so there is a slight indent in the middle. This will avoid the dome effect that rising can cause.

17. Now place a round of baking parchment over the top, but do not press down.

18. Take a baking tin, and line the base with salt before placing your cake tin on top. This layer prevents too much browning on the base of the cake.

19. Place in the middle, or lower, of the oven. Turn down the temperature slightly and cook for the first hour at 150°C / 300°F, Gas mark 2 and then lower to 135°C / 275°F. Check the cake with a skewer after 5 1/2 hours total baking.

20. After baking, remove from the oven, and leave for 1/2 hour before turning out onto a wire rack to cool. Leave out uncovered overnight, then double wrap in greaseproof paper until you are ready to use.

The Grande Finale - Christmas Dinner

The First Course – Soup

Consommé with Quails Eggs

This glamorous soup is light but full of flavour. Serve two quail eggs per person. This soup will serve 6.

Ingredients:

- 1 cooked chicken carcass, skin and fat removed
- 1 onion, skin on, halved
- 1 carrot, washed and roughly chopped
- 1 celery stalk, washed and roughly chopped
- 1 whole garlic clove, skin on
- Small handful fresh tarragon
- Large handful flat leaf parsley, leaves and stalks
- 1 bay leaf
- 3 egg whites
- 2 - 3 drops gravy browning (optional)
- Salt and pepper
- 12 quail eggs

Directions:

1. Place the chicken and vegetables into a large pot with the herbs, and bring to the boil.

2. Reduce the heat, and simmer for around 2 hours.

3. Strain the stock through a large colander, and bring back to the boil, leave to simmer, and reduce by about a 1/4.

4. Cool the liquid in the refrigerator. Skim any fat and impurities off the top of the jug. Then add the egg whites, whisking all of the time.

5. Put back on the heat, keep whisking, and your egg whites should form a crust. Add a couple of drops of gravy browning if you want a richer, darker soup.

6. Line a sieve with muslin.

7. Spoon the crust into the ladle, and then gently spoon the liquid onto the crust.

8. Patiently leave the soup to drip through. Do not be tempted to squeeze.

9. Leave in the fridge until ready to serve.

10. When you are ready to serve, reheat to warm, not hot, and then decant onto a large soup tureen. Cover whilst you prepare the quail eggs.

11. Quail eggs are difficult to break, so gently cut a notch with a serrated edge, then break each egg into boiling water. Try to do 6 at a time. Boil for 2 minutes, remove with a slotted spoon, and then rest the spoon on kitchen paper. Place into the tureen. Cook the second lot of eggs, and then serve to the table.

12. Serve warm, not hot.

The Second Course – Entrées

(For my American Friends, entrées are actually starters, the "entry" into the meal, not the main course)

Entrées were a chance for the kitchen staff to shine. More often than not they were made with cheaper cuts, or offal, but far from being seen by the aristocracy as cheap cuts, the fine preparation of an entrée was a delicacy.

Attention to detail should always have been lavished on the appearance of an entrée because in some ways, it was the most exquisitely presented of all the dishes. It was a fanfare of what was to come, and they were more often than not very colourful as well as tasty. Not only was the objective to tickle the taste buds, but also to stimulate conversation and open up chatter between guests.

Like the main course, or the Remove, as it was more correctly termed, the entrée was invariably served with a sauce. Potatoes too, were often served, but never as boiled potatoes as we would serve today, but in dozens of creative and attractive ways.

Little would the Earl and Countess have expected that by just a decade later, entrées were, for all intents and purposes, a thing of the past. By the outbreak of World War II, it was no longer considered fashionable to serve such banquets, and the entrée was the course that was phased out.

Jugged Hare

Hailing from the same family as rabbits, hares are larger, faster, and in my opinion faster. This dish is still a firm favourite in rural England. But since hares are not, h as plentiful as rabbits, the smaller beast is often supplemented.

Although now usually made with rabbit, which is more readily available. Of course, now most of us rely on the butcher to provide the meat, but I feel sure that the game keeper and Mrs. Patmore, regularly came to "Some kind of agreement." Hares and rabbits are terrible pests, destroying vegetable gardens and so often the promise of a hare needed for the pot was the perfect opportunity for the Game Keeper to get his own back on the carrot munching trouble makers. So popular was this dish in the twenties, if the gamekeeper could not supply, I daresay Mrs Patmore wouldn't be averse to a hushed backdoor conversation with the local poacher either!

The recipe uses dripping, which inspired great memories of my Grandmother. Dripping, the juices and fat from the previous day's roast beef, were collected into a cup and retained for a meal like this. That is, unless someone sneaked into the pantry and smeared it onto a thick crust of bread...delicious!

Ingredients:

- 1 hare
- 4 oz (115g) bacon
- 2 onions
- 1 leek
- 2 pieces of celery
- 2 oz (50g) dripping
- 1 oz (25g) flour
- 11/2 pts (680ml) stock
- 1 wine glass of port
- 3 or 4 cloves
- Lemon juice
- Bunch of fresh herbs from the garden
- Salt and pepper

Forcemeat balls

Directions:

1. Joint the hare, cutting it into neat pieces. Wash thoroughly under the cold tap, ensuring all the blood is gone.
2. Melt the dripping in a skillet, and fry the bacon gently till slightly browned. Remove the bacon from the pan.

3. Now add the hare, and fry over a hot heat until it goes brown. This caramelisation makes all the difference to the dish.

4. Wrap the herbs and cloves in a small piece of muslin to make a bouquet garni. If you can't find any fabric, stick the cloves into one of the onions, and tie the herbs together.

5. To the hare and bacon and vegetables, as well as the bouquet garni, add port and lemon juice, and pour over the stock. Bring to the boil and season to taste. Reduce to a low simmer, to cook for 2 1/2 - 3 hours.

6. About half an hour before serving, mix the flour with water to a runny paste and add to the pot.

7. Gently fry the forcemeat balls to go golden brown.

8. When the hare is cooked, remove the herbs and cloves and drop in about 12 forcemeat balls and cook for a last 1/2 hour.

9. Serve on a large, warmed plate, with the forcemeat balls surrounding the hare and lashings of rich redcurrant sauce.

Devilled Kidney's

Ingredients:

- 6 small lambs' kidneys
- 10 fl oz (275 ml) red wine
- 2 oz (50g) butter
- 1 large chopped onion,
- 1 crushed clove of garlic
- 4 and chopped rashers of unsmoked bacon with the rind and fat removed,
- 12oz (350 g) dark-gilled mushrooms
- 1 level Tbsp flour
- 1/2 level tsp fresh chopped thyme
- Salt and freshly milled black pepper

Directions:

1. Fry the onions lightly in a skillet.
2. As they start to brown add the mushrooms and bacon and fry for 10 minutes until soft.
3. Meanwhile prepare the kidneys.
4. Remove the skin and snip out the white cores with a pair of kitchen scissors.
5. Add the kidneys to the pot, along with the garlic,
6. Cook until starting to brown

7. Sprinkle in the flour to soak up all the juices you can find, don't worry if it sticks a little. Add the thyme.

8. Add the wine.

9. Deglaze the pan, using a wooden spoon and try to get all the caramelised meat from the bottom and into the sauce

10. Bring to the boil and then reduce to a simmer to cook for 15 minutes with a lid on.

11. Remove the lid to reduce the stock for 10 minutes more

12. Serve with potatoes or crusty bread.

The Main Course

Roast Turkey

The turkey was often chosen as the main event as it was very expensive to buy. It was the ultimate grand gesture of the Christmas Meal. It would have been served with a sauce such as bread or cranberry sauce.

In the spirit of authenticity, buy your turkey from the local butcher, not only will it taste better and be a more sustainable option, you can also ask him to let you have the neck and giblets to make your gravy.

Mrs Patmore did not have the stress you and I might have trying to keep it cool because we can't find a space in the refrigerator. Her secret was so obvious I have started to do it myself. In England it is cold at Christmas so the bird was placed in a huge pan of cold water and left outside. Not only does this keep the bird safely chilled it also makes it deliciously moist too. For extra flavouring add an onion, 10 peppercorns and a carrot to the water. Leave outside overnight, with a lid on and out of the way of foxes.

To be true to the period, you should stuff the sausage meat into the cavity, but modern wisdom suggests cook and serve separately for safer eating.

Ingredients:

(Cooking times are based on a 14lb (6.3kg) bird. You need to start cooking 5 hours before you plan to serve the dish.)

- 1 turkey
- 5-6 slices of fatty bacon
- 1/2 pint (225ml) of chicken stock
- Chestnut stuffing
- Fat for basting
- 2lb (900g) of sausage meat
- Bread or cranberry sauce

(Now my grandmother always taught me, roast your turkey on its side so all the juices run into the breast and over the years this has served me very well. The key to this is to place the turkey in the tray, put your hands on top and lean with all your weight onto the bird so it back breaks, then it's easy to get into the oven.)

Directions:

1. Stuff the chestnut stuffing into the neck.
2. Truss the turkey securely with string.
3. Smear as much fat, I use butter, as you can over the turkey. Lay your bacon over the back and cover with foil or greaseproof paper.
4. Place into a preheated oven.
5. Cooking times are: 40 minutes to cook the stuffing properly at 220°C / 425°F Gas mark 7

6. Then reduce to

7. 170°C / 325°F Gas mark 3, for 3 1/2 hours.

8. After cooking for 3 1/2 hours remove from the oven, pour off excess juices, and remove the paper/foil. Return to the oven and cook for a further 40 minutes. Use a skewer or sharp knife to pierce the thigh. When the bird is cooked, the juices will run clear. Remove from the oven and cover. Leave in a warm place (the kitchen work surface on Christmas day will be warm enough!) and let the bird rest for 45 minutes. The meat will relax and the juices will flow back into the meat.

9. Meanwhile make the gravy.

Roast Goose

Below stairs, the food would still be sumptuous as of course there would be plenty of feasting on the leftovers from upstairs. The main course however, would be goose. A rich bird, but far more economical than the lavish turkey

Ingredients:

- 1 Goose
- Fat for basting
- 1/2 Tbsp flour
- 1/2 pt (225ml) stock

Directions:

1. Stuff the body of the goose with sage and onion stuffing.
2. Truss and place in a baking tin with an ounce of fat.
3. Cover the breast with a piece of greaseproof paper and roast at 190°C / 375°F Gas mark 5 for about 1 1/2 - 2 hours
4. About 20 minutes before it is ready, remove and sprinkle the breast with flour and baste with the hot juices from the pan. This gives a rich brown crispy skin. Return to the oven.

5. When cooked, remove from the oven and leave to the rest covered with foil for about 1/2 hour for the juices to return to the meat.

6. Pour off the juices from the pan, into a saucepan and thicken with a little corn flour.

7. Boil and simmer for around 5 minutes and place in a sauceboat beside the goose.

8. Serve on a hot plate garnished with lots of parsley.

Stuffings

Forcemeats and stuffings were designed to accompany and enhance the flavour of the dish. Often their ingredients were chosen not only for taste but also for their reputations of aiding digestion. It is important, then, that the flavours be subtle and not overpower that of the bird. They can seem fiddly to make but are worth the effort in the final result.

Your skill as a cook here is going to be to judge the consistency. You may need to add a little less egg than described or to slacken with a little milk or water. There is no way to guess till you come to combine the ingredients

Chestnut stuffing
Ingredients:

- 1 lb (454g) Chestnuts
- 2 oz (50g) butter
- 3 oz (85g) breadcrumbs
- 1 large egg
- Stock or water
- Nutmeg
- Pepper and salt

Directions:

1. Using a very sharp knife (and minding your fingers), make slits in the shells of the chestnuts, and roast for

around 20 minutes. I like to do this on Christmas Eve on the open fire. Roast them until the outer shell comes away easily.

2. Then drop them into a simmering pan of stock or water, and let them cook till soft.

3. Strain and rub the chestnuts through a sieve.

4. Stir in the breadcrumbs, melted butter, and the beaten egg. Season with a good scraping of fresh nutmeg, and a good grinding of salt and pepper.

Apple Stuffing

(Serve with pork or goose)

Ingredients:

- 1 lb (454g) Sour apples
- 2 1/2 oz (70g) Long Grain Rice
- 1 Egg
- 1 oz (25g) Sugar
- 1 oz (25g) butter

Directions:

1. Wash the rice well, boil until it goes very soft, almost mushy, and then strain.
2. Peel and core the apples.
3. Cut into tiny, thin pieces, and simmer in a small amount of water. Just add enough to stop the apples from burning and sticking.
4. When the apples are soft, add the rice, butter, sugar, and beaten egg.
5. Combine well.
6. Either stuff into the bird or rolled leg of pork, or fashion into balls and roast.

Sausage forcemeat

Ingredients:

- 1/2 lb (225g) sausage meat
- 1/4 lb breadcrumbs
- 1 oz (25g) butter
- 1 egg
- 1 tsp each of chopped parsley or sage
- Salt and pepper

Directions:

1. Mix together all of the ingredients, and bind with a beaten egg.
2. Either stuff the cavity of the turkey and truss, or fashion into little balls, and serve alongside the bird.

Sage and onion stuffing

Ingredients:

- 1 lb (454g) onions
- 1/4 lb (115g) breadcrumbs
- 1 tsp crushed sage
- 1 oz (25g) butter
- Pepper and salt

Directions:

1. Peel and quarter the onions. Parboil them in salted, boiling water for 15 minutes.
2. Strain and chop them. Add the sage, breadcrumbs, melted butter, and seasoning to taste.

Potato Accompaniments

(Choose your favourite)

Potatoes baked in jackets

Directions:

1. Wash and dry large potatoes
2. Prick all over with a fork
3. Place in a hot oven 190°C / 375°F / Gas mark 5 for 90 minutes
4. Split in half
5. Scoop out the flesh, and mash with butter and a teaspoon of cream, then serve returned to the jacket
6. Serve wrapped in a table napkin.

Creamed Potatoes

Ingredients:

- 1 1/2 lb (650g) potatoes
- 1/2 pt (225ml) milk
- 1/2 oz (15g) butter
- 1 Tbsp cream
- Salt and pepper

Directions:

1. Peel and slice the potatoes to about 1/4-inch thick.

2. Put into a plan with the milk, and bring to the boil. Season with salt.

3. Simmer slowly for about 20 minutes or until the potatoes are soft.

4. Drain the milk away, and mash the potatoes until smooth.

5. Add butter cream and a pinch of pepper.

6. Mix well.

Duchess Potatoes

Ingredients:

- 2 lb (900g) cooked potatoes
- 2 egg yolks
- 1 egg white
- 2 oz (50g) butter
- 1 Tbsp cream
- Salt and cayenne pepper

Directions:

1. Rub the cooked potatoes through a sieve.
2. Melt butter in a skillet, and add the potatoes to warm.
3. Add the yolks and cream, and season well.
4. Lightly graze with the end of a fork to texture and score them.
5. Brush with egg white.
6. Bake in a hot oven, 225°C / 425°F / Gas 7 for 20 minutes, or until browned.

Roast Potatoes

These are such an indulgent part of the meal, and it's imperative that you get right for the full Christmas effect. The choice of potatoes available would be what was left in the vegetable garden, but if you have any influence on what the head gardener puts in next year, I would nudge him in the direction of King Edwards, Kestrel, or Maris Piper for the very best roasties.

Ingredients:

- 6 lb (2.7kg) potatoes

- 2 oz (50g) semolina

- 1 1/2 lb (680g) goose fat

Directions:

1. Preheat your oven to 230°C / 450°F / Gas mark 8

2. Halve your potatoes, and place them into a pan of cold water. Bring to the boil, and allow to cook for just 5 minutes.

3. Meanwhile, place a roasting tin of goose fat or a blend of half oil and half butter to heat in the oven. Get it as hot as you can.

4. Strain the potatoes, and toss them in the semolina so they are very well coated. Put the top on, and really shake the contents about. Chipping and roughing

them up a little will mean you have that lovely crunchy outside.

5. Toss in the hot roasting tin, but toss carefully because it will spit ferociously.

6. Roast for 50 – 60 minutes turning halfway through. Make these the very last things you take out of the oven to serve. The hotter they are, the crispier they remain.

Florence Potatoes

Like now, truffles were a well sought-after delicacy. The rich earthiness of the mushroom makes this an entirely exquisite dish. Because it can be hard to separate and serve prettily, it is worth using an attractive dish you are happy to take to the table.

Ingredients:

- 6 medium sized potatoes

- 1/4 lb (115g) chopped ham

- ¼ lb (115g) finely chopped mushrooms

- 2 oz (50g) butter

- 2 oz (50g) finely grated parmesan

- 1 Tbsp chopped truffle

- Salt and pepper

Directions:

1. Peel the potatoes, and soak in cold water until you are ready to use.

2. Cut them into slices about 1/4-inch thick, and line the bottom of the dish

3. Make alternative layers of mushrooms, ham, truffles, and potatoes.

4. Season and sprinkle over the cheese.

5. Melt the butter, and pour over the mix

6. Bake in a moderate oven 190°C/ 375°F / Gas Mark 5 for about 40 minutes, or until the potatoes are cooked.

Gratin Cardoons

This enormous thistle with beautiful purple flowers was a must-have in any Edwardian kitchen garden. Sadly, it has gone out of fashion, and whilst you can find it on herb stalls at garden fairs, it is not something you would find in the supermarket.

This recipe can also be made with celery or artichokes if you cannot get cardoons.

Ingredients:

- 1 1/2 lb (700g) Cardoons

- 10 oz (300g) floury potatoes

- 14 fl oz (400ml) milk

- 5 fl oz (150ml) double cream

- 3 1/2 oz (100g) freshly grated Parmesan

- 3 Tbsp breadcrumbs

- 1 Tbsp butter

Directions:

1. Fill a large bowl with water and a splash of vinegar.

2. Cut off any damaged stems. Despite appearances, the inner leaves are far more bitter than the outer. They look inviting, but are really sharp to the taste. We want the softer, outer leaves.

3. Peel the stems with a vegetable peeler, and try to get most of the stringy bits out so you make it slightly less fibrous in nature

4. Cut them into 1/2-in / 1-cm diagonals, and then drop them in the cold water to stop them going brown,

5. Put a large pan of water on to boil. Add another splash of vinegar and a good sprinkle of salt.

6. Drop in the cardoons, and let them boil for 10-15 mins. Taste to test tenderness

7. Now prepare the potatoes. Cut them into similar sized pieces to the cardoons.

8. Place the potatoes in the milk, and cook to creamy and tender.

9. Mix the potatoes, milk, and about 3/4 of the parmesan with the cardoon.

10. Give a twist of salt and pepper.

11. Place into a gratin dish

12. Bake for 40 mins at 180°C / 350°F / Gas mark 4.

Other Vegetable Dishes

Sprouts, chestnuts and bacon
Ingredients:

- 3 lb (1¼kg) Brussels sprouts, trimmed (or if buying pre-trimmed, buy 2 lb/ 1 kg)
- 6 rashers smoked, streaky bacon, cut into bite-sized pieces (or use more, if you like)
- 7 oz (200g) chestnuts
- 2 oz (50g) butter

Directions:

1. Using a very sharp knife (and minding your fingers) make slits in the shells of the chestnuts, and roast for around 20 minutes. Roast them until the outer shell comes away easily.
2. Then drop them into a simmering pan of water, and let them cook for 5 mins. Drain, run under the cold tap until cold, then drain again.
3. Heat a large skillet, add the bacon, and gently fry for 10 mins until crisp and golden. Tip out of the pan, leaving the fat behind. Throw the chestnuts in, and fry over a high heat for about 5 mins until slightly browned. Tip out of the pan.

4. Add the sprouts to the pan with a tiny splash of water, being careful because it might spit!

5. Cover and finish cooking over a medium heat for about 5 mins until just tender.

6. Stir the mix regularly. Uncover, turn up the heat, and then add most of the butter, and sauté the sprouts a final 2 mins.

7. Add in the bacon and chestnuts, season generously with salt and pepper, then serve with the final knob of butter on top.

Baked Parsnips

Ingredients:

- 2 lb (900g) Parsnips
- 3 – 4 oz (100g) soft brown sugar
- 1 1/2 oz (30g) butter
- Pepper and salt

Directions:

1. Parsnips discolour very quickly when exposed to air so peel in cold water.
2. Halve or quarter the parsnips, and place into boiling water.
3. Reduce heat to a simmer, and cook for half an hour.
4. Place into an ovenproof dish and sprinkle with sugar, butter, and a sprinkle of salt and pepper.
5. Bake in a hot oven 220°C / 425°F / Gas Mark 7 for around 40 minutes
6. Baste with the juices regularly. Remove from the oven when golden brown.

Sauces

Bread sauce

In my experience, this is one for the gentlemen at the table. I have no idea why, but they seem to get very excited about it.

This recipe makes a 1/2 pint (225ml) which should be enough for 4-6 people.

Ingredients:

- 2 oz (50g) white breadcrumbs
- 1 small onion
- 2 cloves
- 1/2 pint (225ml) of milk
- 1/2 oz (10g) butter
- 1 dessertspoon of cream
- Cayenne pepper and salt to taste

Directions:

1. Peel the onion, and stud with cloves. Put into a pan of cold milk, and slowly bring them to the boil.
2. Add the breadcrumbs, and simmer on the lowest possible heat until the bread has gone soft, and the sauce thickens.

3. Take out the onion, add some butter, and seasoning to taste.

4. Add the cream at the very last moment before serving in a sauceboat.

What Mrs. Patmore would have loved:

Bread sauce freezes well, so if you want to get a couple of things done ahead, make the sauce, but do not add the cream. Leave that out until you reheat, then stir some cream through for that just-made taste.

Cranberry Sauce

Ingredients:

- 1 quart (570g) of cranberries
- 4 oz (115g) brown sugar
- 1/2 pt (225ml) water

Directions:

1. Wash the fruit, and then place into a saucepan with the water. Bring it to the boil very slowly, and simmer until the berries are soft.
2. Remove from the heat, and strain.
3. Reheat the fruit, add the sugar, and reheat for around 5 minutes.
4. The sauce will thicken as it cools.

What Mrs. Patmore would have done:

Make this ahead of time. It is served cold and improves its taste for being left a couple of days.

Redcurrant Jelly

(Makes 1 litre or 2 lb jelly)

The simplest of recipes made from the fruit from the estate. Many fruity delights would have been canned to preserve the crops, meaning they were ready to improve dishes at a moment's notice. This is used in the Jugged Hare recipes, but is just as delicious served with roast lamb or duck, or melted into gravies to make rich sauces.

The reason this is so easy is there is no messing about with stalks. Place everything into the pan to stew and then simply through a muslin bag to create a clear ruby jelly.

Ingredients:

- 2 lb (900g) Redcurrants
- 2 lb (900g) Sugar

Directions:

1. Place the berries into a heavy-bottomed pan.
2. Squash them as well as you can to release the juices.
3. Slowly bring to the boil, then add the sugar.
4. Boil fast for 8 minutes

5. Meanwhile, wash your jars and lids. Boil the lids for 5 minutes, and place the jars into a hot oven to dry and sterilise. (Mind how you remove them!)

6. Make a muslin bag by lining a sieve with fabric and placing over a jug.

7. Pour the redcurrant concoction through, and leave it to drip. The more you force it through, the cloudier the jelly, but of course it makes more too, so decide which suits you best.

8. Pour into pots, cover with wax discs when cooled. Put the lids on, and label with satisfaction. Store in a cool, dry place until needed.

Turkey gravy

To make your stock, use the neck and giblets, if possible. Otherwise use normal chicken stock. If you have a modern Teflon-covered roasting tin, you may want to do this in a saucepan to avoid ruining your coating.

Directions:

1. Remove your bird from the tin, and set aside to rest.

2. Place the tin onto the hob and add 1 Tbsp cornflour. Stir it well with a wooden spoon, and scrape away all the meat juices from the bottom of the pan. Gradually add the stock, stir into the flour well.

3. When all the stock is added, bring to the boil to thicken, stirring continuously.

4. Serve in a gravy boat alongside the turkey

Note from Mr. Carson: Please, can you have extra on hand in case the guests would like more?

Desserts

Charlotte Russe

This lovely recipe actually comes from Lisa Heathcote, the food stylist who prepares all of the food for the Downton Abbey episodes. It makes a delectable and light alternative to the heavier pudding, which might have been eaten as a dessert to lunch.

In effect we build this dessert upside down. We start with the orange jelly, which when served is like a stained glass window to view the fruit which has been cut into exquisite little shapes. Take a selection of cookie cutters and cut as many different small shapes as you can. I love the effects of tinned peaches alternated with candied or crystalised angelica stems. If you apply pressure to your peaches, you can flatten them very well which makes cutting shapes much simpler to do. To turn out the pudding, Mrs. Patmore would soak a tea towel in hot water and wrap it around the outside of the tin. The warmth very quickly makes the pudding slide easily away from the sides.

To decorate, place the pudding onto a plate, and pipe pretty cream patterns around the edge. Place carved flowers of fruit around the base. Carefully tie a festive ribbon around the cake.

Ingredients:

- 4 bananas
- 1 pint jelly (454ml) lime or orange (unset)
- 1 packet of sponge boudoir biscuits
- 1/2 pint (225ml) double cream

- Decoration: angelica, cherries, candied peel, apricot halves, or other fruit
- Cake tin (works best if you use a spring form tin)

Directions:

1. Cover the base of your cake tin with cling film to make it easier to release when it is set. Keep it as smooth and flat as you can.

2. Pour a layer of unset jelly into the bottom of the cake tin, keeping it nice and thin. Place into the fridge to set.

3. When the jelly has set, create some shapes with your fruit. Lay them into a pattern on top of the jelly.

4. Whisk the cream to a very soft peak, and mash the bananas.

5. Mix the rest of your jelly with the bananas, and then whisk them together. Fold the banana mixture into the cream.

6. Now line the outside of the cake tin with the sponge fingers, standing vertically, to make a picket fence effect. You might want to requisition a spare pair of hands to help you with this bit, because it is very fiddly. Pour the cream mixture very gently into the middle being careful not to disturb the fingers.

7. Put into the fridge to set for at least four hours or preferably overnight.

Christmas Pudding

The spectacle of the feast was traditionally made on Stir-Up Sunday, the first Sunday before Advent, or the last, or penultimate Sunday before Christmas, depending on how the dates fell. This gave the pudding plenty of time to mature, and of course, plenty of booze added to it too!

Traditionally, the pudding would be steamed for many hours and then would have a second steaming to get it ready to serve. To stop the pudding from drying out, a round of flour dough was placed over the pudding, which would keep the steam locked firmly in.

Rather than making one big pudding, this makes four good-sized ones, meaning you place them along the table, and have a really stunning trail of dishes of blue flames.

Ingredients:

- 3/4 lb (340g) breadcrumbs
- 1/2 lb (225g) flour
- 3/4 lb (340g) suet
- 1 lb (454g) raisins
- 1/2 lb (225g) sultanas
- 1/2 lb (225g) currants
- 1/2 lb (225g) candied peel
- 4 oz (115g) glacé cherries
- 1 finely grated cooking apple
- 6 large eggs

- 1/2 a grated nutmeg
- 1/2 tsp cinnamon
- 1/2 wineglass of stout or porter
- 1/2 wineglass of brandy or sherry
- 1/2 lb (225g) sugar
- Salt

Directions:

1. Wash and chop the fruit. Mix all the dry ingredients together in one bowl; that is, the flour, suet, sugar, spices and salt. In another, drench the fruit with the alcohol, add the eggs, and stir well. Bring the two mixes together, and stir well.

2. Cover, and leave in a cool place to absorb the flavours overnight.

3. Separate into 4 bowls.

4. Make a dough round from flour and water and place it over the top of the pudding.

5. Put a round of grease proof paper over it.

6. Take a muslin cloth, and soak it in hot water, then ring out. Cover it in flour so it will not stick.

7. Place the muslin over the pudding basin, but do not lay it flat because this will stop your pudding rising. Instead make a pleat, of about an inch, in the middle

to give it room to breathe. Fasten securely into place with a piece of string.

8. Now place the puddings into a large pan, and fill with water. Boil for 6 hours. Keep topping up the water every now and then.

9. When they are done, remove the cloths, greaseproof paper, and flour dough. Wrap in greaseproof paper and foil until Christmas Day.

10. To get ready to serve, place another flour dough over the top, replace the greaseproof paper and cloths. Steam for 2 hours.

11. Serve flaming with brandy, then drench with custard, or brandy butter.

12. To get your pudding to flame, the secret is to use warmed brandy. Do not boil it as the vapours will be lost. Carson would use a small silver ladle to cover the pudding and set it alight just before it entered the room. Garnish with holly.

Brandy butter

Mrs. Patmore would create her brandy butter using castor sugar, a finer confectionary sugar than normal granulated. If you cannot get this, use icing sugar.

Ingredients:

- 4 oz (115g) castor sugar
- 2 oz (50g) butter
- 1/2 wineglass of brandy.

Directions:

1. Cream the butter and sugar together until they are pale, light, and fluffy.
2. Whisk in the brandy.
3. Place into a covered bowl, and put in the fridge to set.

Brandy Sauce

Ingredients:

- 2 oz (50g) butter
- 2 oz (50g) plain flour
- 1 pint (570ml) milk
- 2 oz (50g) caster sugar
- 4 Tbsp brandy

Directions:

1. Melt the butter, and stir in the flour.
2. Gradually add the milk little by little, stirring all the time.
3. Bring to the boil, and then simmer it on the very lowest heat for 10 minutes.
4. Add the sugar and brandy, and serve with Christmas pudding.

Mince Pie

This recipe is a very ancient one taken from Mrs. Beeton's cookbook and contains real meat. Ideally, you would make the mincemeat as little as two days before but preferably as much as two weeks. Because the meat takes longer to cook, this works best as one large pie.

The pastry is a standard sweet crust.

Ingredients:

For the filling:

- 2 cups (450g) finely chopped beef suet
- 3/4 cup (130g) currants
- 3/4 cup (about 3oz / 75g) finely chopped rump steak
- 1/2 cup (175g) raisins
- 1/2 cup (85g) packed dark brown sugar
- 2 Tbsp brandy
- 1 1/2 tsp chopped candied citron peel
- 1 1/2 tsp chopped candied lemon peel
- 1 1/2 tsp chopped candied orange peel
- 1 tsp fresh lemon juice
- 1/4 tsp grated nutmeg
- 1 1/2 Granny Smith apples, cored and finely chopped
- Grated zest of 1/2 lemon

Pastry

- 8 oz (225g) plain flour
- 4 oz (110g) butter
- 3 oz (80g) sugar
- 1 large egg

Directions:

1. Mix all of the filling ingredients together, stirring well, and then transfer into a quart jar (1kg jar if you are using metric). Cover and refrigerate for up to two weeks.

2. On the day of making your pies, prepare your pastry.

3. Mix the butter and flour together to make very dry breadcrumbs, add the sugar, and then bind together with the egg.

4. Draw together into a dough, being careful not to overwork, then place into a bag, and rest on the fridge for an hour.

5. Roll out 2/3 of the pastry, and line your pie dish. Retain the rest for the lids.

6. Place about 1 Tbsp of the mix into each one. Glaze the edges of the cases with water to help the lids stick.

7. Cut out the lid, place onto the pies, and crimp the edges.

8. Bake for 1 hour at 180°C / 350°F / Gas Mark 4.

Sweetmeats

Candied Satsumas

Ingredients:

- 12 Satsumas
- 3 cups (775g) of sugar
- 3 cups (775ml) of water

Directions:

1. Bring the water and sugar to the boil. Reduce to a simmer, stirring continually until all the sugar has dissolved.
2. Meanwhile peel the Satsumas
3. Remove the syrup from the heat, and add the Satsumas. Coat well with the syrup, and leave overnight.
4. Next day, remove the oranges with a slotted spoon, and place onto a heated baking tray.
5. Place under the broiler on a medium heat, and let the syrup crisp and go very slightly browned.

6. Turn regularly. You might find a pair of tongs are useful here.

7. Leave to rest for around 2 hours.

8. Serve cooled, at room temperature.

Champagne Truffles

Ingredients:

- 2 cup heavy cream
- 8 ounces semisweet chocolate chopped finely
- 1/4 cup plus 1 Tbsp (250ml) Champagne
- 1 Tbsp Cognac
- Coarse sanding sugar for rolling

Directions:

1. Place the chocolate into a bowl.
2. Heat the cream to just boiling, and then immediately pour over the chocolate. Mix well, then add in the champagne and the cognac.
3. Refrigerate until the mixture is just firm enough to be able to roll into ball.
4. Line a baking sheet with greaseproof paper.
5. Mrs. Patmore would use a melon baller to get evenly sized chocolates.
6. Scoop out the chocolate mix, and roll into careful balls.
7. Roll in the sugar to get a beautiful frosting over the sweet.
8. Place each one carefully onto the baking sheet.
9. Cover carefully with cling film.

10. Refrigerate for at least half an hour, but these can be made up to 3 days before.

11. Serve in tiny pretty bowls on a bed of sugar.

12. The perfect end to your Christmas Meal.

Your Menu in French

For complete authenticity, ensure your menu is
scribed in French. Here are your translations.

Breakfast	Petit Déjeuner
Brawn	Museau
Kedgeree	Pilaf de Poisson
Luncheon	Déjeuner
Raised Game Pie	Tourte à la viande
Afternoon Tea	Jeu de Tarte Eclatée
Mince Pies	Tartelette de Noël
Mince Meat	Haché de Viande
Pastry	Pâtisserie
Christmas Cake	Gâteau de Noël
Christmas Dinner	Repas de Noël
Consommé with Quails Eggs	Consommé d'Oeufs de Caille
Entrées	Entrées
Jugged Hare	Civet de Lièvre
Devilled Kidney's	Rognons à la Diable
The Main Course	Le Plat Principal
Roast Turkey	Dinde Rôtie
Roast Goose	Oie Rôtie
Stuffing	Farce
Chestnut stuffing	Farce aux Marrons
Apple Stuffing	Farce aux Pommes
Sausage forcemeat	Farce de Saucisses
Sage and onion stuffing	Farce d'Oignons et Sauge

Potato Accompaniments	Garniture de Pommes de Terre
Potatoes baked in jackets	Pommes de Terre en Robe des Chan
Creamed Potatoes	Pommes de Terre à la Crème
Duchess Potatoes	Pommes Duchesses
Roast Potatoes	Pommes de Terre Rôties
Florence Potatoes	Pommes de Terre Florence
Gratin Cardoons	Gratin de Cardons
Sprouts, chestnuts and bacon	Germes, Châtaignes et Bacon
Baked Parsnips	Panais au Four
Sauces	Sauces
Bread sauce	Sauce à la Mie de Pain
Cranberry Sauce	Sauce aux Cramberries
Redcurrant Jelly	Gelée de Groseilles
Turkey gravy	Jus de Dinde
Desserts	Desserts
Charlotte Russe	Charlotte Russe
Christmas Pudding	Pudding de Noël
Brandy Butter	Beurre au Cognac
Brandy Sauce	Sauce au Cognac
Mince Pie	Tartelette de Noël
Sweetmeats	Friandises
Champagne Truffles	Truffes au Champagne

Conclusion

So as the last embers of the fire are dying, and you begin to yearn for a doze, it is time to retire to bed. The festivities are over for another year.

Tomorrow though, unlike us, the Crawleys will not have to worry about finding homes for all the new toys. For them, beautiful life will continue. The beautiful swan of a house will continue to glide elegantly through to the next great banquet. Mrs. Patmore and Daisy will doubtless be preparing dishes anew.

If you have enjoyed the feast, and smiled a few times, then just one final tip on etiquette. Every well-bred lady would always pen a few words to say thanks to her host. For a review, please feel free to post your comments here.

Please do come again soon. It is so lovely to spend time with you, and I am sure Mrs. Patmore and Daisy will continue to cook up a storm!

In fact, won't you join us for Tea at Downton, tomorrow afternoon? Or perhaps we could make an appointment for you to come Dining at Downton next week.

Either way, thanks so much for joining me, and I hope to hear from you again soon.

Elizabeth Fellow

Check out these other Books by Elizabeth Fellow...

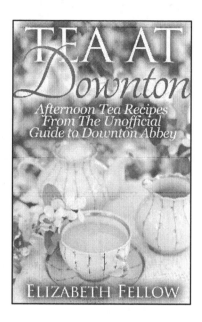

(http://www.amazon.com/dp/B00I5ASVX0)

(http://www.amazon.com/dp/B00J914MMS)

(http://www.amazon.com/dp/B00KJKF8DU)

28070646R00055

Made in the USA
San Bernardino, CA
20 December 2015